The Tropical Rainforest

The Tropical Rainforest

Les Hiddins

PUFFIN BOOKS

Contents

Our Tropical Rainforest   1
Rainforest Layers   2
Rivers, Creeks, Waterfalls   4
Trees and Vines   6
Rare Plants, Air Plants   8
Survival in the Rainforest   10
Bush Foods   12
Bush Fruits   14
Beans and Nuts   16
What's in the Water?   18
In the Treetops   20
Birds Below   22
Flying High   24
Flying Foxes and Bats   26

Rainforest Creatures   28
Rainforest Frogs   30
Snakes and Lizards   32
Creeping, Crawling   34
Exploring the Rainforest   36
What's it Called?   38
Glossary   39
Index   41

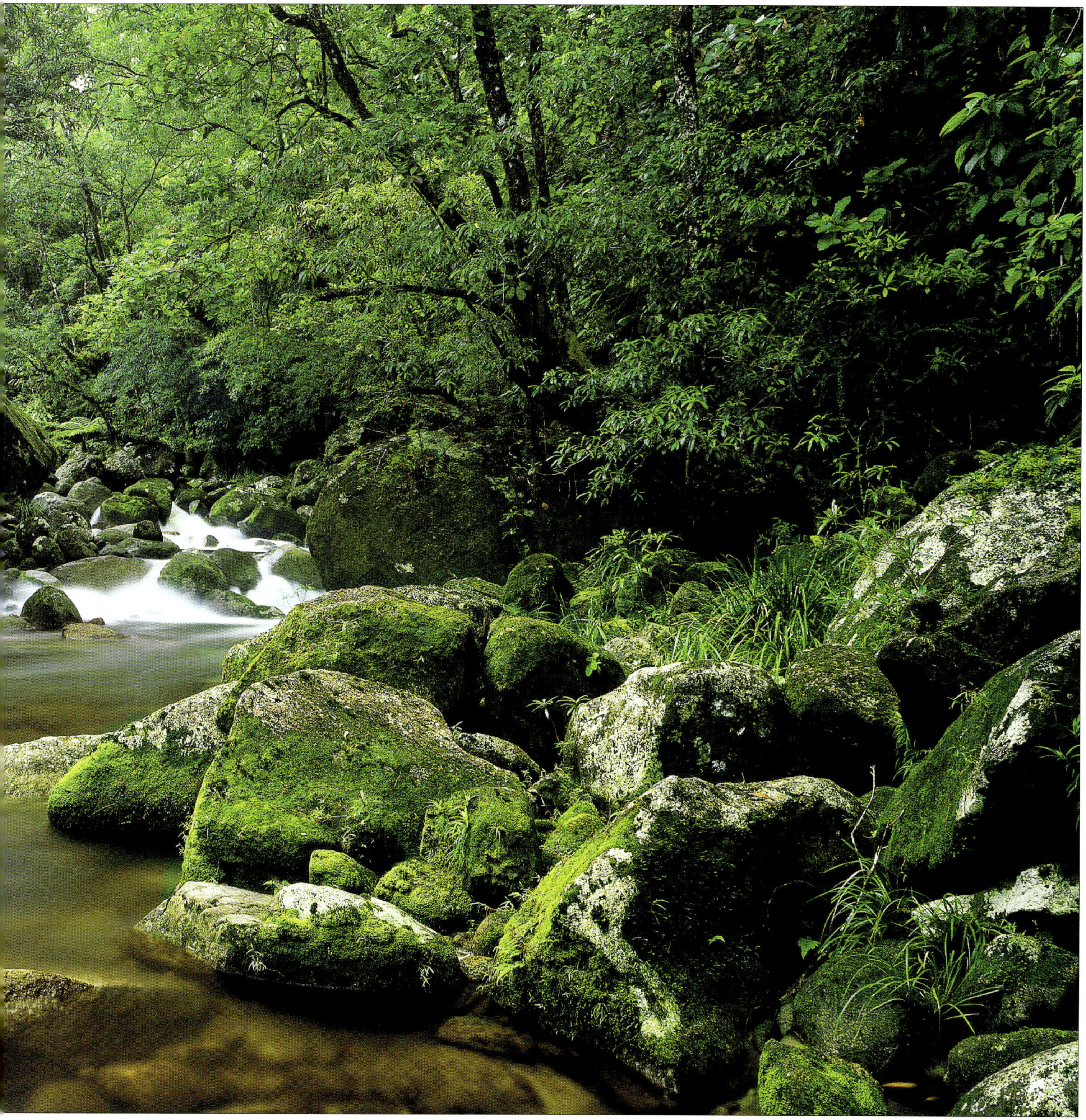

Our Tropical Rainforest

Australia's tropical rainforest takes up a tiny part of our vast country. Millions of years ago, the entire continent was covered in rainforest. These days, the rainforest stretches from just north of Townsville up to Cooktown on Cape York. There are a couple of small pockets further north on the Cape. And that's all. Yet in these areas there are trees you don't see anywhere else in Australia. There are plant species that are millions of years old. There are rare birds and unique animals. It's really quite a special part of the world.

Daintree National Park, northern Queensland

Warning
Some bush foods are poisonous. Never handle or eat any bush tucker without checking with an adult if it's safe to do so.

Words printed in **bold** are explained in the Glossary on page 39.

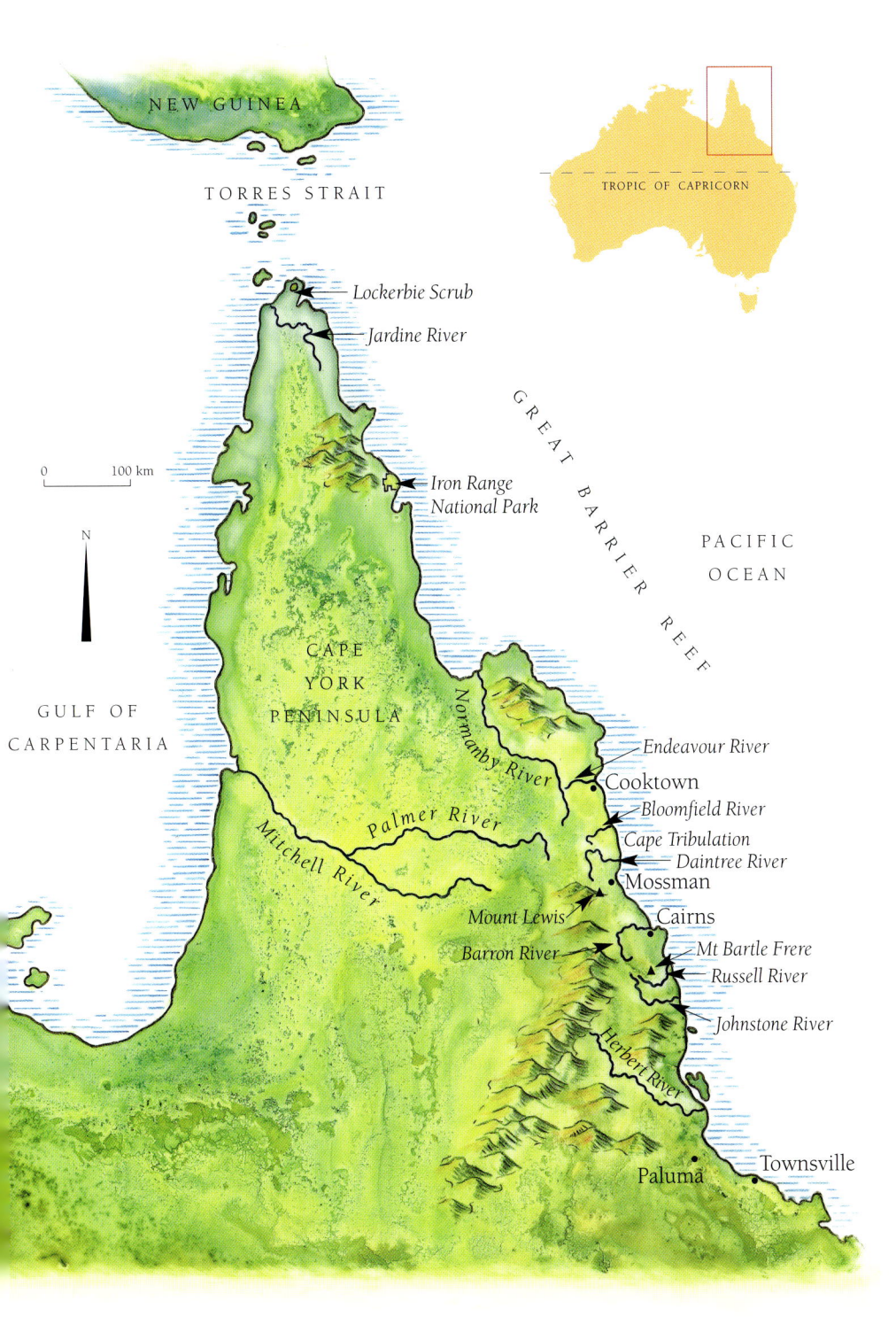

WHAT IS A RAINFOREST?

Broadly speaking, there are tropical, sub-tropical and temperate (or cooler) rainforests. The type of **vegetation** they have varies, but extremely heavy rainfall and lush, dense growth of plants and trees are common to them all. Tropical and sub-tropical rainforests have higher temperatures and heavier rainfall than temperate ones.

Tropical Rainforests

Tropical rainforests are found near the equator, between the Tropic of Capricorn and the Tropic of Cancer. These rainforests are very warm, very wet and very humid. They cover only one-sixth of the world's surface, yet they contain more than half of the world's plant and animal species.

> Australia's largest area of tropical rainforest, from Paluma to south of Cooktown, used to be called the 'big scrub'.

Rainforest Layers

Tropical rainforests have several layers, or levels, although it's not always easy to tell where one level finishes and another starts. The **canopy**, like an umbrella, blocks out almost all the sun. Very little sunlight reaches the forest floor and it's difficult for plants to grow there. When a giant tree crashes down, often bringing others with it, there's a break in the canopy and light can get through. In that sunlit patch, young trees, lawyer vines, wild raspberries, wild ginger and other plants quickly grow. At every level, plants are struggling to reach the sun.

The understorey
Banana bushes, native gingers, tree ferns, palms and smaller trees grow here. Ferns and other plants sprout from tree trunks. Birds and ants nest in the **understorey** and small lizards and geckoes, stick insects, beetles, bees, moths and many butterflies call this level home.

The forest floor
This level is a tangle of roots, with moss and **lichen**, a thick layer of **litter**, dead and decaying leaves. The forest floor is alive with beetles, cockroaches, centipedes, leeches and other creatures. Small animals like bandicoots and some birds, such as scrubfowls and cassowaries, scratch around, feeding and nesting.

Leaves, fruits and other **debris** constantly fall to the rainforest floor.

The canopy

High above the understorey, the treetops form the rainforest canopy. Thick, woody vines and creepers drape over trees. Flowers such as orchids and mistletoe cling to branches and tree trunks. Much more sunlight reaches this level and many plants have fruit and flowers. Dazzling butterflies, flying foxes, and birds like parrots and pigeons feed here. Some animals, like tree-kangaroos, rarely come down from the canopy.

Giants at the top

At the top – dotted around – are the tallest trees, or **emergents**, towering above the rainforest canopy. They might reach 50 or 60 metres. They receive plenty of sunlight, but are exposed to high temperatures, strong winds and heavy rains.

Rivers, Creeks, Waterfalls

In the rainforest, water drips off leaves, spills over rocks, rushes along creeks and crashes down waterfalls. Rainforest country is damp, humid and often soggy under foot. When it rains, it really dumps down, with torrential rainfall and great big drops of water. In many parts of the forest, however, only a small amount of the rain penetrates the canopy and reaches the rainforest floor. On a rainforest track, where there's a break in the canopy and the rain can get through, it soaks the ground.

HOW MUCH RAIN?

In these areas, rain can be measured in metres, not just millimetres. On average, between about 1200 mm and 4000 mm of rain falls each year in our tropical rainforest. That's 1.2 metres to 4 metres of rain. Just south of Cairns is Mt Bartle Frere, the highest mountain in the tropical rainforest and one of the wettest places in Australia. Up to 9000 mm (or 9 metres!) of rain has been known to fall here in a year.

Rain drain

Most of the rain falls during the Wet season, from around December to March. Sometimes there are **cyclones**, bringing incredibly strong winds and even more rain. The rain tends to run into **gorges** and **gullies**, through rivers and creeks.

Drip tips
Many rainforest leaves have developed 'drip tips', long points that let the rain run off quickly. If the leaves stayed wet, moss and **algae** could grow on the leaves and harm the plant.

Waterfalls
Waterfalls are a spectacular feature of the rainforest landscape, especially after heavy rains. At Wallaman Falls, the waters from Stony Creek plunge almost 300 metres over a cliff into a riverbed below. This is one of Australia's longest waterfalls.

Over the years, water has worn away the rock at Josephine Falls in northern Queensland.

All the rivers run
The tropical rainforests of northern Queensland have enormous river systems like the Russell and the Johnstone and the Barron, which run all the year. During the Wet season many rainforest rivers and creeks flood.

Trees and Vines

The astounding number of plants in the rainforest **environment** means there's quite a bit of competition – for space and for sunlight. Trees grow to enormous heights, reaching for the sun, sometimes stretching for 20 metres or more before the branches spread out. You also find vines, or lianas, climbing and clinging, weaving and reaching upwards. When the long vines get to the top of the trees, they spread across the canopy. Sometimes the vines become so heavy, the trees can't take the weight and crash to the ground.

Going up
Some vines use hooks to cling as they climb. Others curl around trees, while still others grow small springy tips that wrap around trees and other vines as they climb towards the sun.

Buttress roots
Some rainforest trees (right) develop huge, above-ground roots called buttress roots. These roots might reach 9 metres or more in height and spread along the ground. No one's exactly sure why the roots are like this. They may help spread the weight of the giant trees, because the soil and the underground roots are shallow.

Strangler figs
The soft fruits of the strangler fig trees are a favourite with birds and fruit bats. Bird or bat droppings, containing the fig seeds, often fall on the trunk or in the fork of a tree. In no time at all, the seeds sprout, the shoots grow upwards and the roots stretch down towards the ground.

Gradually the fig branches wrap around the trunk and strangle the tree. The tree's leaves die, the trunk rots away – and the strangler fig takes its place.

Strangler fig

Beware the stinging tree

The giant stinging tree might be the most dangerous thing you'll come across in the rainforest apart from the wild pigs. The leaves, branches and even the twigs can give you a very serious sting. And it lasts for weeks – sometimes months.

The huge, heart-shaped leaves are covered with very fine hollow hairs. When the hairs stick into the skin they stay there, and release a poison. The trees have a fruit, like a mulberry. You can eat the berries, but my advice is to stay away!

SHIELDS AND LONG SWORDS

Rainforest Aborigines carved shields from buttress roots. They also used hardwood from rainforest trees to make huge 'swords'. No other Aboriginal people used anything like these swords. Something must have influenced these rainforest people. Perhaps they met very early explorers, who came long before Europeans settled here. No one really knows.

Shield
Length: 89 cm

Sword
Length: 143 cm

Rare Plants, Air Plants

Many plants have found special ways of surviving in the rainforest environment. In order to get closer to the sunlight, some rainforest plants grow on the side of trees. They're called **epiphytes**, or air plants, because they get most of their water from the moisture in the air. They do not harm their 'host' tree. They get their food from the litter that falls from the canopy above. The litter turns to mulch and fertilises the plant.

On the trunk
Flowers and fruit grow directly on the trunk and main branches of some rainforest trees, which makes it easier for birds, butterflies or fruit bats to find them in the shadowy forest.

The flowers and fruit of the bumpy satinash (*right*) grow directly on the tree trunk.

AIR PLANTS
Moss and lichen, ferns such as elkhorns and staghorns, and many orchids are epiphytes. Some epiphytes are small, others grow to impressive sizes.

Orchids
Orchids grow on the ground at the edges of the rainforest and also on trees, or in fern baskets. Their waxy petals hold water. The flowers' colours and strong smell attract birds, butterflies and bees. Their long roots dangle down, soaking up moisture from the air and they also store water in swollen stems that look like bulbs.

King orchid

FUNGI

Fungi grow in weird and wonderful shapes on the rainforest floor. Unlike almost all other plants, they don't need sunlight to grow. They put out fine, white threads, like roots, to collect their food. These threads also help the leaves and debris to break down, or **decompose**.

Maiden veil fungus

This strange plant is called a stinkhorn fungus because of its terrible smell. The stem usually appears overnight, then a lacy 'maiden veil' skirt spreads out. A foul-smelling, sticky slime quickly attracts flies. By the next day the plant has shrivelled and started to rot away.

Dangerous glow!

Some fungi are luminescent – they glow in the dark. It's quite surprising at night to see this stuff glowing. Some fungi are colourful, some are smelly, most are poisonous.

Hanging gardens

As elkhorns and crow's nest ferns grow on the side of trees they form a 'basket', which hangs out from the trunk, catching rainfall, leaves and other debris. After a while, this plant matter breaks down and creates enough soil for other plants, like orchids, to start growing.

Survival in the Rainforest

In some ways, living in the tropical rainforest was not as tough for Aboriginal people as surviving in the desert country. There was more food and it was often easier to find. Still, quite a few plants were poisonous and could only be eaten after extensive preparation, which could sometimes take days. People also need more than food to survive. Aborigines had to find shelter and medicine, tools and weapons from the forest around them.

If you walk beneath a green ant nest, the ants sense your body heat. They will drop on you and give you a very sharp bite.

BUSH MEDICINE
Toothache, burns, stomach aches and infected sores were just some of the illnesses Aboriginal people treated using plants from the rainforest.

Stop the sting!
The thick, sticky sap from the cunjevoi *(below)* was sometimes used to ease the pain of the giant stinging tree *(see page 7)*. It was also used to relieve snake bite, stings from insects and stingrays.

Cunjevoi

Wait-a-while
Lawyer vine is very common all through the rainforest, or scrub country as it's often called. It has a **frond** like a palm frond, but a very fine one. The tendrils wave around in the air, looking for something to lock onto. If you get too close, it will grab you with its small hooks and it takes a while to untangle yourself. That's why some people call it 'wait-a-while'. Rainforest Aborigines used the lawyer vine in many different ways.

Green ants nest

Green ants

GREEN ANTS

Green ants make their nests by matting together leaves still hanging on trees. The worker ants use the silk made by the larvae to join the leaves.

Green ant medicine

Aboriginal people ate green ants just like a snack. Sometimes they ate the **larvae** from the nest. It has a pleasant, lemony taste. The Aborigines would also pound the ants and larvae together and mix it with water to make a lime-flavoured medicine. This was rubbed on the chest, or sometimes drunk to relieve colds, headaches and sore throats.

USING THE CANE

Lawyer vine was a very important resource for Aboriginal people in the rainforest.

The flexible lawyer-vine canes with their sharp hooks were used to snag freshwater crayfish, and to extract witchetty grubs from their holes in rotten logs.

Shelter

Rainforest Aborigines used the lawyer-vine cane to make an igloo-shaped hut. They covered this frame with the leaves from the banana palm or the fan palm. It was simple but provided good cover, especially in the Wet season.

Lawyer-vine baskets

The strong canes were also used to make fish and animal traps. The canes were split and woven into baskets or 'dilly bags', which were used to carry things, or to soak poisonous plants.

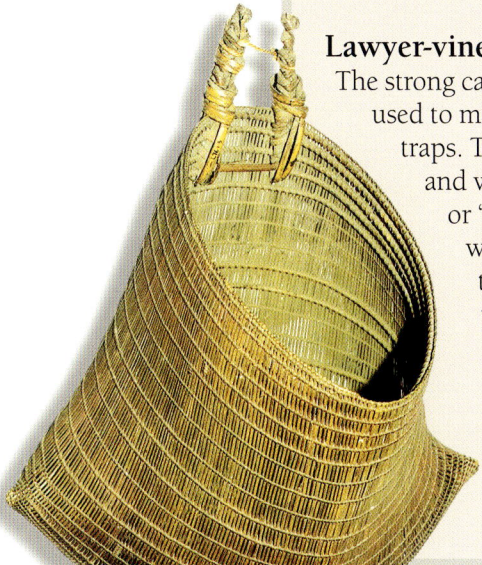

Aboriginal basket
Length: 30 cm
Width: 38 cm

11

Bush Foods

Gathering and hunting for bush tucker was shared by the whole Aboriginal community in the rainforest. Women collected most of the day-to-day food. They dug for yams, gathered fruit and nuts, grubs and eggs. It was their job to remove the poisons from certain plants, so that the plants were safe to eat. The men were responsible for hunting lizards and snakes, wallabies, possums, scrubfowls and other animals. Rainforest Aborigines also caught eels, yabbies, fish and shellfish from the rivers and sometimes along the coast.

Eggs for dinner
Scrubfowl (*above*) and brush-turkey eggs were considered excellent tucker. These birds build large mounds and bury their eggs to incubate them. Aboriginal people would push a spear or a piece of lawyer-vine cane into the mound and poke around. If the spear came back dripping with egg yolk they knew there were eggs in the mound. The Aborigines would then dig into the mound of rotting vegetation, bugs, ticks and worms. Later, the eggs might be cooked on a fire, or just eaten raw.

Wild ginger
Wild ginger can often be seen growing beside a track or stream, in a little bit of sunlight. Aborigines used to chew the berry seeds, which have a slightly ginger–pepper taste. They also used the long leaves to wrap food before cooking it.

Collecting eggs
Around the base of the Cairns fan palm (*right*) is a wrapping like loosely woven material. Small birds often used this for nesting and Aboriginal people knew to look there for eggs. Sometimes they'd use the fibre to wrap the eggs before carrying them.

YAMS

A yam is like a swollen root, or tuber. Yams were a staple food for Aboriginal people and finding and digging for them was an important skill.

'Long yams' have big, heart-shaped leaves on the vine. The yam itself is long and hairy. Sometimes the yams were eaten raw, but mostly they were roasted on hot coals. They taste like sweet potato.

Snake supper

Aborigines would catch scrub pythons, or amethyst pythons, then singe the scales off. They'd coil the snake, skewer it with splinters of lawyer-vine cane, put it on hot coals, and cook it for about an hour. The white flesh looks a bit like chicken meat. The eggs were a special delicacy.

Scrub python
Length: up to 8 metres

Bush Fruits

Australia's tropical rainforests contain a remarkable variety of native fruits in all colours, shapes and sizes. And as rainforest trees and bushes grow fruit at different times, there are always new fruits ripening and falling to the forest floor. Fruits were a valuable part of the traditional Aboriginal rainforest diet. Of course, Aborigines had to compete with the birds, possums, flying foxes and other native wildlife that also feast on the fruit.

RASPBERRY JAM
Prickly wild raspberry bushes (*right*) often grow beside creeks and tracks where there's a little extra sunlight. The small berries are dry but slightly sweet. Early European settlers in the rainforest areas used those berries to make jam. The berries don't last long – the birds love them.

BLUE QUANDONG
The majestic quandong tree usually grows beside rivers and creeks in the rainforest. You will often see the bright blue fruit being carried along waterways and streams. The small, marble-sized fruits can be eaten raw and have a slightly sour taste. Quandongs are not particularly nutritious.

BUSH BANANAS
Bush bananas usually grow on the edge of the rainforest and along riverbanks, where there's sunlight. The fruit looks just like a banana you might buy in a shop, except smaller. Inside the banana, however, there are lots of black seeds – more seeds than **pulp**.

Aboriginal people would eat the pulp, which is slightly sweet and sticky. Sometimes they'd eat the flowers. They'd also cook and eat the central part of the trunk and the ground shoots.

14

CLUSTER FIGS

These figs grow in big clusters along the trunk and main branches of the fig tree. They're quite small, with masses of seeds, but they don't have much of a taste.

APRICOT FIGS

These little figs, which turn red when ripe, aren't much bigger than a pea. They're packed with small seeds and have a pleasant, sweet flavour.

RAINFOREST PLUMS

Big bunches of purple plums droop from the branches of the Davidson plum tree, mainly during the Wet season. The leaves and plums have fine, irritating hairs that need to be wiped off. It's worth it though. The juicy, dark red flesh is sour but very tasty.

Beans and Nuts

The majestic tropical rainforest trees often have large – sometimes huge – seed-bearing pods. Some pods contain beans or nuts, which are very tasty. Others are quite poisonous. We don't know how Aboriginal people worked out what was safe to eat. Maybe they used a method of trial and error over many, many years. One thing's for sure though, the way a plant or a food looks can be very deceptive. Never eat any bush food without checking if it's safe to do so.

Blackbean
Length: pod, 10–25 cm

DEADLY!
Aboriginal people found ways to remove the poison from some plants so that they could be eaten. This often meant pounding the beans into a pulp and soaking the pulp in running water for several days, before finally cooking it.

BLACKBEAN
When the pods of the blackbean split open, they look like miniature canoes. The large beans inside are *extremely* poisonous. Aboriginal people would remove the poison, make the pulp into 'flour' and then bake it into a type of damper.

Blackbean flowers

16

NUTMEG

Native nutmeg trees often grow beside rainforest creeks or near rivers. The fruit, or pod, looks like a rusty brown capsule. When the fruit splits open, there's a hard seed inside. Surrounding the seed is a fire-engine red cover called mace. The seeds can be ground up or grated to provide the spice called nutmeg. The mace can be eaten as well.

Nutmeg
Length: pod, 3–4 cm

CANDLE NUTS

You often see candle-nut pods lying on the rainforest floor. The pods, which are tough to crack, contain up to four nuts. The raw pulp tastes superb – very similar to a macadamia nut.

Burning brightly

Early settlers and miners sometimes used the nuts like candles. They'd thread them on wire and heat them. The nuts have a high oil content so when they burn they give off a slightly sooty, candle-like flame. And that, of course, is why we call them candle nuts.

Candle nut
Width: pod, 4–8 cm

Aboriginal people sometimes used the trunk of the nutmeg tree to make dug-out canoes.

MATCHBOX BEAN

The giant matchbox bean, which grows on a vine, looks harmless but the flesh is poisonous. Rainforest Aborigines prepared the beans so they were edible. They had other uses for the matchbox bean too.

Fish poison

The bark and stem of the matchbox-bean vine were soaked and crushed in water to make a soapy mixture, or lather. It could then be washed in small pools of water to poison the fish. It works quite well, too. The fish would float to the surface and could be easily caught. The lather could also be used as a soap or shampoo.

Matchbox bean
Length: pod, 1 metre or more

What's in the Water?

All through the rainforest country there's a network of creeks, rivers and streams. These waterways traditionally supplied rainforest Aborigines with a reliable source of food – and **protein**. There are jungle perch, catfish, yabbies, freshwater crayfish and more. For people living near the rainforest coast, there was a good supply of ocean fish, turtles, stingray and crayfish. Rainforest Aborigines mainly used vine and fish nets to catch fish. Sometimes they used fish poisons (see page 17), little fish traps or spears.

SNAKE-NECKED TURTLES
Most of the freshwater turtles found in rainforest waterways are small snake-necked turtles. They tuck that long neck in an S-shape under the shell, or carapace. Turtles sometimes sun themselves on a rock or log during the day.

Northern snake-necked turtle
Length: up to 40 cm (shell)

SLIPPERY EELS
Eels are long slender, snake-like fish that tend to burrow in the mud or sand. Just about every rainforest creek and river north of Townsville has eels in it. They grow up to 2 metres long. They're slippery and they have razor-sharp little teeth.

Eel traps
To catch eels, Aboriginal people would make a trap like a perfect long stocking. They might use the fibre from a palm tree and lawyer-vine cane. They'd put the bait down one end of the trap. The eel would go in to get the bait and get caught, as there wasn't enough room for the eel to turn around and swim out.

Eel trap woven from lawyer vine
Length: 110 cm
Width: 14 cm

Turtle tucker
Turtles were eaten as bush tucker all over northern Australia – in some Aboriginal communities they still are. They were cooked in an earth oven or placed whole upside down on hot coals. Once the turtle was cooked, the bottom 'plate' was easily removed. The meat is oily with a strong chicken-like flavour.

FRESHWATER SHELLFISH

Freshwater yabbies, or freshwater crays, grow quite large and are surprisingly tasty. They were usually caught in traps. The crays tend to **hibernate** in mud burrows from June to August. The unique bright blue and red river crayfish, known as Mount Lewis crayfish (*below*), are only found in some of the rainforest mountain streams. Those giant pincers are used to attack other crayfish.

Yabby
Length: up to 15 cm

Pulling in prawns

To catch freshwater prawns, Aborigines would trail a lawyer vine, with its sharp hooks, in the water. When the prawn tried to eat it, the vine was pulled in quickly and the prawn would be hooked. The prawns turn bright pink when cooked, and taste like saltwater prawns.

Freshwater prawn
Length: up to 6.5 cm

Mount Lewis river crayfish
Length: up to 30 cm

In the Treetops

Millions of years ago, the island of New Guinea was joined to Australia. In the tropical rainforest, especially in the mountains and near the top of Cape York, there are rare bird species that cannot be found anywhere else in Australia. They can be found, however, further north in the tropical rainforests of New Guinea. They are a link with our almost-forgotten past. Birds live at every level in the tropical rainforest. The huge number of insects, bugs and worms, and the rich variety of plants mean that the birds aren't all competing for the same food.

PAPUAN FROGMOUTH
These birds have a big, wide flat bill, a long tail and bright red eyes. Their huge mouths are a yellowish colour inside. Frogmouths live on the edge of rainforests, mainly in the understorey. At night they feed on beetles and other insects. Although they're not very good hunters they sometimes catch small lizards and frogs.

Bird or branch?
The frogmouth's mottled greyish-brown feathers provide a clever camouflage. During the day, especially if frightened, these birds straighten their head in line with their body and 'freeze'. They do a pretty good imitation of a broken branch.

Papuan frogmouth
Length: 48–56 cm

Fishing trip

Bright violet-blue little kingfishers perch quietly on branches overhanging rainforest streams, watching for movement, before quickly diving in to get their food. They fly low and fast over the water.

When it's time to nest, they use their long sharp beaks to make a tunnel into a mud bank, or even into a termite mound. The female then lays its eggs in a little chamber at the end of the tunnel. This is Australia's smallest member of the kingfisher family.

RARE PARROT

Iron Range, on Cape York, is the only place in Australia you'll see the beautiful eclectus parrot. The male is bright green, with flashes of red under the wings. The female is brighter still – crimson red and blue. These parrots tend to fly high over the rainforest canopy, and make a loud screeching cry.

The parrots nest in deep hollows in trees, usually at the edge of the rainforest, close to water. They feed on the blossoms, fruits and seeds of the canopy trees.

Eclectus parrot
Length: 33 cm

Little kingfisher
Length: 11 cm

WHAT'S THAT NOISE?

Some birds in the tropical rainforest make very strange noises. The spotted catbird makes a wailing sound like a cat. And the large-tailed nightjar, or 'waterpump bird', makes a chop-chop sound just like a waterpump.

Birds Below

Some of Australia's most unusual birds live on the tropical rainforest floor. The rainforest, especially around the Daintree River area, is home to the rare cassowary. These huge, flightless birds look like something from the age of the dinosaurs. The rainforest is also home to two remarkable birds known as megapodes, or 'big feet'. The scrubfowl and the brush-turkey use their powerful feet to scrape the rainforest litter into a giant **mound**, like a big compost heap, to **incubate** their eggs.

BRUSH-TURKEY

Instead of making a nest, the male brush-turkey builds a huge mound up to 4 metres across and 2 metres high. The female digs a hole in the mound and buries her eggs there. She may keep adding eggs for a few months. The male guards the mound fiercely, chasing away any intruders.

What's the temperature?

The brush-turkey sticks his head in, as far as his yellow **wattle**, and takes the temperature of the mound with his tongue. He keeps the mound at an even temperature by adding or subtracting dirt or leaves.

The eggs take almost two months to hatch. The chicks have to dig their way out of the mound – not an easy job. But once they're out, they're off into the forest. They can look after themselves. Within hours of being born they can fly.

SCRUBFOWLS

Scrubfowls also build mounds, although both males and females look after the mounds. These birds are smaller than brush-turkeys, but their vast nests can be up to 15 metres across and 4 metres high. Often more than one pair of birds will share the mound for nesting.

Orange-footed scrubfowl
Length: up to 47 cm

Australian brush-turkey
Length: 70 cm

SOUTHERN CASSOWARY

These big birds – they might weigh 50 or 60 kilos – have bright blue necks with dangling red wattles and a bony 'helmet' on their head. They don't fly but they can run very fast. They push through the tangled undergrowth, eating fallen fruits, fungi, insects and snails from the rainforest floor.

Cassowary chicks

Cassowary camouflage

The male birds sit on the large green eggs, for seven or eight weeks, to hatch them. The fathers never leave the nest – not even to eat. Then they look after the chicks for about nine months. The cassowary chicks have brown and cream stripes – they don't get the glossy black feathers, or the helmet, for a few years.

Watch out!

Cassowaries are shy but they can be dangerous. They are fiercely aggressive if there are chicks around and are capable of killing a person. Their huge powerful legs have sharp spikes, or claws, on the inside toes. You sometimes hear their deep booming call in the forest.

Southern cassowary
Height: up to 1.5 metres

Flying High

Australia's largest butterfly and the world's biggest moth live in the tropical rainforest. The rainforest environment is perfect for these delicate creatures. It also provides a generous supply of caterpillar food – flowers and fruits and leaves. Caterpillars, which will become butterflies or moths, can eat many times their own weight in food. They are fussy eaters, though, and they need plenty of their favourite food during this important growing stage.

Green spotted triangle butterfly
These butterflies flit nervously around. They rarely stop, but hover over rainforest flowers, collecting nectar. You sometimes see them feeding in the sunlight along a rainforest track.

Green spotted triangle butterfly
Wingspan: 8.5 cm

Birdwing butterfly
Australia's largest butterfly, the Cairns birdwing butterfly, is quite spectacular. The male is smaller than the female and less colourful. In the picture below, the butterfly has just emerged from the **pupa**. Male butterflies wait for the female to emerge and sometimes mate before the female's wings are dry.

Soft but spiky
The spiky black caterpillar of the birdwing butterfly is a strange sight. The spikes are really a bluff – they're quite rubbery and soft. If these caterpillars are disturbed or threatened they emit a sickening sweet smell.

Cairns birdwing butterfly
Wingspan: up to 20 cm (female)

Birdwing caterpillar
Length: up to 10 cm

Flashing blue

Ulysses butterflies feed high in the rainforest canopy, occasionally coming down to gather nectar from favourite flowers. Their brilliant blue wings shimmer in the light. You'll see a flash of blue, but when they close their wings, the undersides are brown and they almost seem to disappear.

Ulysses butterfly
Wingspan: 11 cm

Hercules or atlas moth
Wingspan: up to 25 cm

Giant moth

The hercules or atlas moth is the largest moth in the world. Its **wingspan** of up to 25 cm is bigger than that of many birds. The female is slightly larger than the male. The atlas moth caterpillar is also a giant, growing up to 12 cm in length.

The female atlas moth has no mouthparts. After emerging from the pupa, it lives for just a few days on the fat in its body. It mates, lays up to a hundred eggs, then dies soon after. I reckon that's not much of a life.

25

Flying Foxes and Bats

Large colonies of fruit bats, often called flying foxes, live in the rainforest. These creatures thrive on blossom and fruits. Other bats in the forest are insect-eaters. All bats are nocturnal, flying and feeding at night. During the daytime, you might spot them in their 'camps', hanging from the trees. Mainly, however, you hear them. They make a tremendous noise, squabbling amongst themselves. And there's usually a horrible stench in the air. Each bat species has its own distinct, musky odour.

FLYING FOX OR BAT?
There are two main types of bat. Fruit bats, also known as megabats, eat fruit and nectar from flowers and use their excellent sight and sense of smell to find their way around. The 'other' bats, the microbats, are usually smaller and mainly eat insects. Microbats use a type of radar, or **echolocation**, to find their way around. Both types of bats can be found in the rainforest.

Fruit bats play a key role in the rainforest. Like birds, they help carry pollen to other trees and spread seeds throughout the rainforest.

Queensland blossom-bats
These tiny blossom-bats, shorter than a little finger, are unusual because they tend to roost by themselves. They have a brush-like tongue just right for gathering sticky nectar from flowers. They hover while lapping up pollen and nectar from blossom.

Queensland blossom-bat
Length: 4–16 cm

Black flying foxes
They can be found feeding in the rainforest, although they may set up camp in drier areas or on the edge of the forest. They will fly long distances – up to 50 kilometres – for food. They're one of the biggest of all bats and roost in thick **foliage**, in high trees.

Black flying fox
Length: 24–26 cm

Spectacled flying foxes

These flying foxes are common in the tropical rainforest where you might have between 1000 and 50 000 bats in a camp. During the day they hang from tree branches, often just using one foot, and wrap their leathery wings around themselves. If it's hot they use their wings to fan themselves. Baby bats cling to their mothers' fur with their sharp teeth and claws.

Spectacled flying foxes feed on blossom nectar and pollen as well as fruits like figs and plums.

Spectacled flying fox
Length: 22–24 cm

27

Rainforest Creatures

It's surprising how few animals you see during the day in these rainforests. Most of the creatures are nocturnal, so they're mainly active at night. They live in the trees where it's easy to hide. Some are very shy or secretive. Others are cleverly camouflaged. Once you get further north, into the rainforest areas of Cape York, you're really starting to get quite close to New Guinea. Some animals that are found in our tropical rainforests are also found in the tropical rainforest country in New Guinea.

Lumholtz's tree-kangaroo
Head and body: 48–60 cm
Tail: 60–70 cm

Kangaroo climber

There are just two species of tree-kangaroo in Australia. These rare tree-climbers are only found in small pockets of the mountain rainforest. They're nocturnal and live high in the treetops.

Lumholtz's tree-kangaroo looks like a combination of kangaroo, koala and bear. Their powerful front legs, big paws and very sharp claws are just right for climbing and gripping. The exceptionally long tail helps them balance as they move around the canopy eating leaves and fruits.

Bandicoot

Long-nosed bandicoots hide in a leafy nest on the rainforest floor during the day. At night these small **marsupials** emerge and shuffle through the litter. They poke their long noses around, or dig down, searching for insects, grubs, worms and tasty roots. They leave small, cone-shaped holes in the ground.

Bandicoots carry their young in a pouch. The pouch opens backwards, however, so that when the bandicoots are digging, the young ones aren't showered with dirt.

Long-nosed bandicoot
Head and body: 31–43 cm
Tail: 12–16 cm

RATS!

You might see the native white-tailed rat, which is about the size of a rabbit or small cat, with an appetite to match. They eat insects, bird eggs, fruits, seeds, frogs and more.

Black rats –*Rattus rattus*– introduced by European settlers, are also at home in the rainforest. They sleep by day, and emerge at night to eat whatever they can find.

Herbert River ringtail possum

These possums are only found in mountain rainforest in northern Queensland. The long tail is used like an extra limb, to wrap around branches when climbing. When not climbing, the tail is coiled into a ring. During the day, ringtails usually sleep in a tree-hole.

Herbert River ringtail possum
Head and body: 33-44 cm
Tail: 33–40 cm

Rainforest Frogs

Wet, damp, humid and shady, with an almost unlimited supply of tasty insects – you'd have to agree that the rainforest is just right for a frog. In fact, the variety of frogs in the tropical rainforest is quite astonishing. A few species can *only* be found in these rainforests and nowhere else in the world. You can't always see them, but you can definitely hear them, and the sound is sometimes deafening. Only male frogs make the typical croaking noise, and each species has its unique sound. Frogs only hear the mating call of their own species. Somehow, they filter out all the other frog calls.

Sticky fingers
The orange-thighed tree frog hangs on tightly with its sticky fingers and toes. Tree frogs are rather flabby. The loose skin helps them grip onto slippery trees and shiny leaves.

Orange-thighed tree frog
Length: 6.5 cm

TREE FROGS
They have long, webbed fingers and toes, with round pads on the ends. The pads release a sticky substance that helps them grip onto slippery trees and wet leaves. Tree frogs also tend to have long, strong legs – perfect for leaping and climbing from one branch to another.

What's to eat?
Frogs flip out their long sticky tongues to catch flying and crawling insects. Some bigger frogs also eat small reptiles, like lizards, and small mammals, like mice.

Eye to eye
A frog's big eyes do more than just look around. Frogs swallow their food whole. The eyes create bulges on the inside of the mouth. When the frog swallows food, it blinks, its eyes push down and help force the food down its throat.

WATERFALL WHISPER
The little waterfall frog looks like a slimy rock – it can stay very, very still and is mottled in earthy colours. It clings to the edge of boulders and rocks, surrounded by fast-moving water. It doesn't seem to have a mating call – maybe because it wouldn't be heard over the crashing of the waterfall anyway.

Northern barred frog
Length: about 9–11 cm

DOWN TO EARTH
The northern barred frog spends its time hidden under the leaf litter on the forest floor. You only find them in very wet tropical rainforest. They don't have big round sticky finger pads, like tree frogs – that's because they don't need to cling to trees.

White-lipped tree frog
Length: up to 14 cm

Orange-thighed tree frog

Balancing act
The white-lipped tree frog, or giant tree frog (*above*), is the world's largest tree frog. They're quite graceful as they move around the trees, catching insects. These frogs spend their days hiding in leafy trees, often high in the canopy. When the orange-thighed tree frog (*left*) makes its mating call, its vocal sac swells into a large yellow lump. This may help attract a partner.

Snakes and Lizards

Rare lizards, giant snakes and other **reptiles** lurk in the rainforest country, but they're not that easy to see. Although many are daytime hunters, their **camouflage** makes it difficult to find them amongst the shadows and dense foliage. Bigger reptiles, such as the scrub pythons and goannas, were regularly hunted by rainforest Aborigines.

LIZARD FAMILY
There are five types of lizards – dragons, monitors (often called goannas), geckoes, skinks and legless lizards.

Leaf-tail gecko
I reckon this little creature looks quite ancient. Against a tree trunk, it's almost impossible to detect. Like some other lizards, if grabbed or attacked, its tail will drop off, to distract the **predator**. The gecko soon grows another tail.

The leaf-tail gecko has sharp claws so that it can easily grip tree trunks and rocks, hanging vertically, or even upside down. Geckoes don't have eyelids, but a clear covering to protect the eye. They lick their eyes with their tongue to keep their eyes clean – a bit like a windscreen wiper on a car.

Leaf-tail gecko
Length: up to 14 cm

Greenest python

These rare pythons are only found in a very small area of northern Queensland. By about three years of age, a green python has changed from yellow, or sometimes red or even blue, to a brilliant green colour. Quite magnificent.

By day, they coil themselves over palm fronds or vines. At night, they hunt small mammals, birds, frogs and lizards. They suffocate them, then swallow them whole.

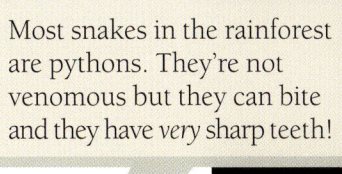

Most snakes in the rainforest are pythons. They're not venomous but they can bite and they have *very* sharp teeth!

Green python
Length: about 1.8 metres

A baby green python hatching from its shell. Snake eggs have a soft, leathery texture.

Longest snake

The scrub python, or amethyst python, is Australia's longest snake. The average size is about 4 metres, but they can grow to 8 metres long. I've seen them stretching right across the road with their tail in the scrub on one side and their head in the scrub on the other side.

At night they hunt bats, rats, possums, bandicoots, birds – and anything else that takes their fancy. Special pits on their face detect heat and help them catch warm-blooded animals, often in complete darkness.

Boyd's forest dragon

These colourful dragons blend perfectly with the rainforest colours and textures. They live in the understorey, eating spiders, crickets and other insects. If disturbed, they stay motionless, clutching the side of a tree. Just their eyes seem to follow you. They look fierce but they're harmless to humans. If in danger, they puff themselves up to look bigger, in order to frighten predators.

Boyd's forest dragon
Length: 51 cm

Creeping, Crawling

Thousands of insect species make their home amongst the damp leaf litter and debris. They chew and gnaw into rotting timber, fallen fruit, dead leaves. They're breaking it down, making it into a type of compost. I guess you could say they are **recycling**. There are also armies of ants at every level of the rainforest, and the canopy is alive with leaf-chewing insects like beetles, and pollen-seeking insects like wasps and bees. And then there are the many spiders, including the big orb-weavers that spin huge, round, or orb-shaped, webs.

Rhinoceros beetle
Length: up to 6 cm

ARMED FOR FIGHTING

Rhinoceros beetles belong to a big family of beetles known as scarabs. Only the male beetles have the impressive 'rhinoceros' horns, and they use them to fight their rivals. They often make a loud hissing or squeaking sound. They're quite harmless, though the claws at the end of their legs can grip surprisingly strongly. The larvae feed in the damp litter on the rainforest floor, helping recycle leaves and other debris.

Black leech
Length: up to 20 cm when filled

BLOOD-SUCKING LEECHES

Leeches, a type of worm, are small and not usually harmful, but they are a nuisance. They pierce the victim's skin, inject a pain-killing fluid that stops the blood clotting, and then suck up the blood. Leeches swell when they take in the blood and can consume up to ten times their body weight in blood.

St Andrews cross spider
These spiders are also orb-weavers, but they weave a zigzag cross-shape into their web. That may catch the light and attract insects or it may help strengthen the web. The large, colourful females tend to stay in the middle of the web, while the tiny males hide near the edge.

The black leech grips a leaf with its powerful, sucker-like mouth, and stretches out in search of prey.

GOLDEN ORB-WEAVER

The females are huge spiders, with a body up to 4 cm long, and legs spanning 9 cm or more. They weave giant, sticky, wheel-shaped webs, usually stretched between two trees. When the light catches the web, the golden thread shimmers. These webs are large enough to catch a skink, a little bird or even a small bat.

A dangerous mate

The female golden orb, up to ten times bigger than the male, will occasionally eat a male partner after they have mated. Sometimes she will only manage to grab a few of her partner's limbs. The male can survive, however, growing new limbs the way some lizards grow a new tail. Here *(right)*, the male hitches a ride on his partner's back.

St Andrews cross spider
Body: 1.5–2 cm

Golden orb-weaver
Female, body: 4 cm long
Leg span: 9 cm

Exploring the Rainforest

Most of the tropical rainforest country has been explored by Europeans who have come looking for treasure of one kind or another. They came searching for land, cutting their way through the rainforest, digging for gold, mining for tin, looking for other minerals. Maybe they didn't realise just what they were destroying. Now we know how fragile the rainforest is. We know that it's taken millions of years to develop and that it's home to rare plants, birds and animals that all depend on each other for survival. If the rainforest goes, so will they.

Captain Cook

Cook was the first English person known to land on the east coast of Cape York, on the edge of the rainforest. His ship, the *Endeavour*, crashed on a jagged coral reef in 1770. His sailors struggled to free the ship and finally put ashore near the mouth of the Endeavour River, about where Cooktown is these days.

While the *Endeavour* was repaired, Cook and famous **botanist** Joseph Banks explored the countryside. They discovered and recorded plants and animals they'd never seen before. They ate plenty of bush tucker – kangaroo, turtle, birds and local plants.

Lady apple, a bush fruit that Joseph Banks wrote about in 1770.

Botanist Joseph Banks who travelled with Captain Cook

Gold rush!

In 1870, a hundred years after Cook landed in Australia, gold was discovered in the Palmer River Valley, in the northern Queensland rainforest. In no time at all, a rush was on and eager 'diggers' headed into the bush in search of gold. They had to carve a track from the coast through the scrub to the goldfields. There was hardly even a path to follow.

The gold only lasted 30 years, but large areas of rainforest were explored, and destroyed, as people tried to make their fortune. The Russell River was – briefly – another rich goldfield.

TIN MINING

In the early 1900s, after the gold rushes, some miners started digging for tin. Around the Bloomfield area, up in the hills, there are still remains of the tin-scratchers' camps and the channels they dug.

A tough life

For those miners life was pretty unpleasant. The scrub was dense, it was wet all the time and they worked under a canvas canopy that cut out the sunlight.

The miners didn't understand the countryside – they didn't even try to. They had to cart in everything, including food, on their backs, or on pack horses. If they'd looked around they might have seen that there was food right there – bush tucker.

Gold diggers working at the Russell River

Diggers prepare to defend themselves on the Palmer River goldfields

What's it Called?

Plants, animals, birds and insects have 'common names' – names we use every day. However, different people sometimes use different names for the same thing. That can be very confusing. So there's also a scientific name, usually in ancient Latin or Greek. That name always stays the same and can be understood anywhere in the world. Here are the common and scientific names of the main plants and animals in this book.

Common Name	Scientific Name
Plants	
apricot fig	*Ficus leptoclada*
blackbean	*Castanospermum australe*
blue quandong	*Elaeocarpus grandis*
bumpy satinash	*Syzygium cormiflorum*
bush banana	*Musa acuminata*
Cairns fan palm	*Licuala ramsayi*
candle nut	*Aleurites moluccana*
cluster fig	*Ficus racemosa*
cunjevoi	*Alocasia macrorrhizos*
Davidson plum	*Davidsonia pruriens*
giant stinging tree	*Dendrocnide excelsa*
king orchid	*Dendrobium speciosum*
lady apple	*Syzygium suborbiculare*
lawyer vine, wait-a-while	*Calamus* spp.
long yam	*Dioscorea transversa*
matchbox bean	*Entada phaseoloides*
nutmeg	*Myristica insipida*
wild ginger	*Alpinia caerulea*
wild raspberry	*Rubus rosifolius*
Birds	
Australian brush-turkey	*Alectura lathami*
eclectus parrot	*Eclectus roratus*
little kingfisher	*Ceyx pusilla*
orange-footed scrubfowl	*Megapodius reinwardt*
Papuan frogmouth	*Podargus papuensis*
southern cassowary	*Casuarius casuarius*
Butterflies, Moths, Spiders, Insects	
black leech	*Amicibdella nigra*
Cairns birdwing butterfly	*Ornithoptera priamus*
golden orb-weaver	*Nephila edulis*
green ant	*Oecophylla smaragdina*
green spotted triangle butterfly	*Graphium agamemnon*
hercules moth, atlas moth	*Coscinocera hercules*
rhinoceros beetle	*Haploscapanes* sp.
St Andrews cross spider	*Argiope aetherea*
ulysses butterfly	*Papilio ulysses*
Mammals	
black flying fox	*Pteropus alecto*
Herbert River ringtail possum	*Pseudocheirus herbertensis*
long-nosed bandicoot	*Perameles nasuta*
Lumholtz's tree-kangaroo	*Dendrolagus lumholtzi*
Queensland blossom-bat	*Syconycteris australis*
spectacled flying fox	*Pteropus conspicillatus*
white-tailed rat	*Uromys caudimaculatus*
Reptiles, Frogs and Fish	
Boyd's forest dragon	*Hypsilurus boydii*
eel	*Anguilla reinhardtii*
freshwater crayfish, yabby	*Cherax* spp.
freshwater prawn	*Macrobrachium australiense*
green python	*Chondropython viridis*
leaf-tail gecko	*Phyllurus cornutus*
Mount Lewis river crayfish	*Euastacus fleckeri*
northern barred frog	*Mixophyes schevilli*
northern snake-necked turtle	*Chelodina rugosa*
orange-thighed tree frog	*Litoria xanthomera*
scrub python, amethyst python	*Morelia amethystina*
white-lipped tree frog	*Litoria infrafrenata*

Glossary

algae	a type of plant that grows in water or very damp places	**larvae**	insects at a stage of growth before they have developed into their adult shape. Sometimes called grubs. Larva is the name for one insect at this stage
botanist	a specialist who studies plants		
camouflage	disguise. When an insect, animal or other object has a similar colour or texture to the surrounds, which makes it difficult to see		
		lichen	a plant that grows like a thick, pale green or brown moss on trees and rocks
canopy	the top layer of leafy branches and creepers that form a thick cover over the rainforest	**litter**	leaves, twigs, fallen fruit and other rubbish on the ground
		marsupial	an animal that raises its young in a pouch
cyclone	a storm with extremely heavy rain, and powerful winds that blow in a circle	**mound**	large heap or pile of dirt, leaves, sand or other material
debris	what is broken and left behind. In the rainforest, broken twigs, branches, leaves, nutshells	**predator**	an animal that hunts another animal to kill for food
		protein	an essential part of the human diet, necessary for healthy growth and development. Food from animals, such as fish, provides better protein than plant food
decompose	to rot or decay		
echolocation	finding an object by using sound waves		
emergent tree	one of the very high trees in the rainforest, which emerge above the canopy		
		pulp	the flesh or inside part of a fruit or nut
environment	the earth, the plants and the temperature in a particular area	**pupa**	the stage in an insect's life between a larva and an adult
epiphyte	a plant that grows on another plant but does not harm it	**recycle**	to treat or change something so that it can be re-used
foliage	the leaves on plants and trees	**reptile**	a cold-blooded animal, such as a snake or lizard
frond	a feather-like leaf, often large, usually of a fern or palm	**understorey**	layer of vegetation between the rainforest floor and the canopy
fungi	plants such as mushrooms and toadstools. Fungus refers to just one of these plants	**vegetation**	the plants, including grasses and trees, in a certain area
gorge	narrow, steep-sided valley, which is often rocky	**wattle**	a fold of skin, often a bright colour, hanging from the neck of some animals, especially birds
gullies	small valleys or deep gutters, usually cut by a stream or other running water		
hibernate	when an animal stays completely inactive during winter	**Wet season**	the rainy season in northern Australia, generally from December to March
incubate	to keep at a warm temperature so that eggs will hatch	**wingspan**	the width across from the tip of one wing to the tip of the other wing

THE TROPICAL RAINFOREST

Project Editor and Manager
Margaret Barca

Managing Editor
Astrid Browne

Design
Tony Palmer, Penguin Design Studio
and Sandy Coventry, P.A.G.E. Pty Ltd

Special thanks to
Carol Hiddins; May Abernethy;
Fay Donlevy (Indexer); Ray Pask
(Geography Consultant); Tony Orr;
Bruce Rankin (map illustration);
Kay Ronai (Editor); ANT Photo
Library; Cape Tribulation Tropical
Research Station; Museum of
Archaeology and Anthropology,
James Cook University (Townsville)
for permission to reproduce artefacts
from their collection; National Library
of Australia, for permission to
reproduce historic images;
Nature Focus, Australian Museum;
Queensland Wildlife and Fisheries.

PUBLISHER'S NOTE
The author and publisher cannot
take responsibility for any illness,
injury or ailment brought on through
consuming or handling plants.

The Publisher also wishes to thank
Tourism Queensland for providing
images of northern Queensland for
THE TROPICAL RAINFOREST.

PHOTO CREDITS
Abbreviations

AG	Andrew Gregory
ANT/	ANT Photo Library: Kelvin Aitken (ANT/KA), G B Baker (ANT/GB), D & V Blagden (ANT/D&VB), J Burt (ANT/JB), Brian Coates (ANT/BC), Andrew Dennis (ANT/AD), Frithfoto (ANT/F), K Griffiths (ANT/KG), Martin Harvey (ANT/MH), I R McCann Photo (ANT/IRMP), Ralph & Daphne Keller (ANT/R&DK), Ted Mead (ANT/TM), N H P A (ANT/NHPA), Michael O'Connor (ANT/MO), C & S Pollitt (ANT/C&SP), Otto Rogge (ANT/OR), G E Schmida (ANT/GS), A P Smith (ANT/AS), B G Thomson (ANT/BT), Klaus Uhlenhut (ANT/KU), Dave Watts (ANT/DW), Keith Williams (ANT/KW)
AUS/GT	Auscape (Glen Threlfo)
GL	Glenn Leiper
JM	John Meier
LH	Les Hiddins
LI/DJ	Living Image (Darren Jew)
MA	May Abernethy, James Cook University
NF/	Nature Focus: H & J Beste (NF/H&JB), John Cann (NF/JC), Keith Lindsay Fisher (NF/KF), Norman Chaffer Estate (NF/NCE), Michael Trenerry (NF/MT), Robert Valentic (NF/RV)
NLA	National Library of Australia
PBA/SS	Penguin Books Australia (Steve Strike)
TAM/DE	Tropical Australia Media (Dick Eussen)
TM	Ted Mead
TQ	Tourism Queensland

Abbreviations for positions
t – top; b – bottom; l – left; r – right; c – centre; fp – full page

Front cover: *Ulysses butterfly*, TQ; *Les Hiddins' Akubra Sombrero*, PBA/SS; *Les Hiddins*, PBA/SS; *Narrow leaved lilly-pilly*, AUS/GT; *Livistonia palm*, LI/DJ; *Red-eyed tree frog*, NF/RV. Half title page: *Hercules moth*, ANT/F. Title page: *Les Hiddins*, PBA/SS. Contents pages: *Ulysses butterfly*, TQ; *Les Hiddins*, PBA/SS; *Atherton Tableland*, ANT/TM. Back cover: *Millstream Falls*, ANT/JB.
Pages vi ANT/KA (t), TAM/DE (b). 1 PBA/SS. 2 ANT/TM (t), TAM/DE (b).
3 ANT/NHPA (t), ANT/F (r), ANT/TM (b). 4 ANT/AD (t), TQ (b). 5 JM (fp),
PBA/SS (b). 6 AG (l), TM (r). 7 ANT/OR (l), LH (t), DA (c), DA (b). 8 TAM/DE (t),
ANT/F (l), ANT/GS (b). 9 ANT/MO (l), ANT/GS (r). 10 PBA/SS (t), LH (l), LH (r).
11 LH (t), ANT/KU (c), DA (b). 12 ANT/R&DK (t), GL (b). 13 TM (fp), LH (t),
ANT/R&DK (b). 14–15 LH. 16 TAM/DE (l), LH (r). 17 ANT/KW (t), PBA/SS (b),
LH (r), LH (l). 18 NF/JC (l), DA (r). 19 LH (t), LH (r), NF/JC (b). 20 NF/H&JB (l),
ANT/F (r). 21 NF/H&JB (t), ANT/BC (b). 22 ANT/KG (l), ANT/BT (r). 23 TQ (fp),
NF/NCE (t). 24 LH (t), ANT/F (l), ANT/F (r). 25 TQ (t), ANT/F (fp). 26 ANT/AS
(l), NF/H&JB (b), PBA/SS (r). 27 TAM/DE (fp), ANT/MH (c), ANT/GB (r).
28 ANT/KG (b), ANT/DW (t). 29 ANT/R&DK. 30 NF/MT. 31 ANT/AD (t),
ANT/GS (b), ANT/R&DK (r). 32 ANT/D&VB. 33 PBA/SS (l), ANT/F (t),
ANT/C&SP (r), TQ (b). 34 ANT/AD (l), NF/KF (r). 35 ANT/IRMP (l), ANT/F (r).
36 Rex Nan Kivell Collection, 13129, NLA (t), Rex Nan Kivell Collection, 13153,
NLA (l), LH (b). 37 Illustrated Australian News, NLA (b), NLA (r). 38 NF/MT.
39 LH.